CHUCK'S LIFE

Charles M. Daily Jr.

CONTENTS

FROM THE BEGINNING

I was born Charles M. Daily Jr. on November 28, 1970 at 7lbs. 11oz. and 20" long. I was born from proud parents Charles M. Daily Sr. and Diane M. Daily in Jersey City, New Jersey (Hudson County). We lived in East Windsor for about two years. My two step brothers, Allan and Steven, were eight or nine years older than me, and big sports fans. We lived there until I was about two years old.

After that, my family and I moved into a four bedroom ranch in Beachwood, New Jersey. When I was about four years old, my brother Shawn D. Daily was born the day after Christmas. It was good times, but since we were four boys, it was probably hard for my parents at times.

My dad ran heavy equipment and was gone most of the day, and my mom worked at the local hospital. Growing up was good. I spent a lot of time with family and my parents' friends. My dad's best friends were Uncle Nicky and Aunt Pat. They had three girls and three boys, and we did a lot of growing up. We would go fishing, camping, have parties, and other family functions. Then there was Victor, my dad's fishing buddy—they were always at the dock in Beachwood trying to catch something. My father had three sisters and one brother we'd visit and get togetherwith very often: Susie, Barbra, Trudy, and Uncle Wayne. All together, we were twelve cousins. We lived very close until I was about nine years old. Then, my dad's sister Susie, Uncle Frank and their four girls moved to Florida, the Sunshine State, when I was eleven years old. We would go on many family trips down south to visit as Shawn and I were getting older.

My Uncle Frank was a New York City bus driver for over twenty years. He flew up weekly to work until his death—questioned on how and why it happened. He wasn't happy being away from his girls and wife for long periods of time, including traveling every week. It was a sad situation for the whole family, especially for the girls and my father —seeing his sister in pain destroyed him. They were extremely close.

My Aunt Barbra lived in upstate New York by the Catskills with her two boys, Billy and David, and her two daughters, Holly and Jenny whom I was close to as well. My Uncle Wayne, Aunt Teddy, the two boys and my cousin Kimmy, who has Down Syndrome, lived the closest to us. Then there were my Aunt Trudy, Uncle Ray and my cousin Gracie, who lived up north from us—don't know exactly where, but it was about an hour and a half drive from us. They also eventually moved to Florida for their retirement. When they all lived close, my family always made time for visits—it was important to my parents.

My father's mom, Grace, lived up in the Catskills Mountains. She was the most amazing woman I ever met. She did everything by herself. The house was on the side of a mountain where was

3

a huge horse farm at the top, and down the hill across the street was a trout stocked stream that went for miles. It was very laid back. My father always wanted to move there, but my mom was a city girl and wasn't having it. Grandma Grace passed away when I was thirteen. I had never seen my father cry so much in his life; he was devastated. Unfortunately, I never got to meet my grandfather. Only saw pictures of him.

My mom Diane M. Daily had one best friend, Barbra Roche. I still talk to her today. Her husband is Dave and their son David. They were our neighbors and the best ones you could ask for. My mom had one sister, Dottie, and two brothers, Al and Johnny. Uncle Al was in the Navy when we were growing up and lived in Texas with his wife Valerie. He wound up spending over thirty years in the service. My Uncle Johnny, who also had Down Syndrome, was the kindest person you would ever meet even though my grandfather Dominick treated him like an animal at times. Uncle Johnny still had a loving mother and sister to protect him. Grandma

Anita, who was nothing but 4'10" tall, was a little Italian woman who made the best homemade pizza I've ever eaten in my life. She always cherished her son and kept him safe until the day he died at age 54. Anita was my mom's step mother, but was always a big part of our family growing up.

She died at 98 years old.

Then there was grandma Josephine and grandpa Stanley, my mother's real mom and step dad who treated my grandmother like a queen. They lived in North Bergen until I was about fifteen years old, then they moved down the street from our house so that my mom and dad could help them out more. She had the most beautiful house up north with a huge Christmas tree out front. My brothers and I were always climbing on it—a big Cherry Tree and grapevines all around the back yard. It was like a fairytale playground for us. The whole basement was a kitchen area with an old school bar and cool trinkets everywhere. It was my dream house as a kid; it had everything. I was heartbroken and happy at the same time when they sold it. We spent many holidays there growing up; it was like our second home. I remember watching Willy Wonka there when it first came out and still think about the house every time I see it on TV. Growing up had its ups and downs, but all in all, I wouldn't change the family times.

THE TEENAGE YEARS

Becoming a teenager was a blessing in itself. I remember my neighborhood friends were Kenny, Tommy, Billy, Herbie, Timmy, and Carl, who were the kids I played football, soccer, and yankee pirate with. I loved it. Ray, Victor, and Dom were kind of the trouble maker kids of the neighborhood, but nonetheless were a really good part of my life. Dirt bikes, pranks, sledding, and rock-and-roll were their things to do, and I always joined in for the ride. Mix Master Mike and Bobby "Big City" Ellis were my neighborhood homies who were into rap and freestyle music like me.

All the neighborhood kids were nice growing up. Some played sports together, some played music, some rode bikes and dirt bikes, and some we always got in trouble with, but yet always respected one another and always got along. In the winter, we would go to the corners of Tiller Ave and Bowline where there was a big hill for sledding. The sleds we had were the old-school ones with the metal blades under them. We used to make five-foot snowballs and block the streets from cars passing through. We would have huge snowball fights at the bus stop before school. Some kids would play catch with a baseball while waiting for the bus, and the kids who lived right at the corner wouldn't come out of their houses until the bus pulled up.

Everyone pretty much got along, even though we were all into different things. Growing up was a blast. I remember in 7th grade, when breakdancing was a thing, meeting my first black friends: Thomas Banks, Steve Scott, and my brother-from-another-mother, Oscar Cradle aka Bogey, who were all close to me through high school.

In 8th grade, this brother and sister who were new to the area came walking out the library steps at Intermediate West wearing their matching bomber jackets looking all B-Boyish. His name was Rorre and hers was Julie. Both wound up being life long-friends of mine and friends with others I met along the way. Rorre was the funny kid around—he knew how to put a smile on everyone's face.; even if you didn't want one, you couldn't resist laughing your ass off. He always had the best dance moves and loved listening to club music. He was a one-of-a-kind friend that still makes me smile every time I think about him. Unfortunately, Rorre passed away in early 2021 at age 50.

Being a teenager was hard, especially in school. I was always the biggest kid in every class. Had the biggest feet and was a little goofy at times, but tried fitting in wherever I could. Every coach wanted me for basketball and football, but I wouldn't get much play time compared to the other kids, so I would quit the team and move on. My passion was music and becoming a DJ one day, but that didn't work out either. Still to this day I spin whenever I have a chance—probably the only 50-year-old with 12 crates of records and two turntables. The best advice I give my kids and other people is to follow your dreams when you're young and see where it leads you. Something I never did. I always lived in the moment and had no plan. That's one of my regrets—not following my passion as a teenager.

Starting high school was weird. Most of the people I grew up with were finding new friends and parting their ways in other directions. Some I ran into once in a while, some I didn't see anymore, but that's when new friends came along like my boys, Roger Cender, Adam, Kevin, Eric, Carlos, Eddie, Billy T. and a whole bunch more that I was close to throughout the years.

In junior year I started getting into cars. My first car was a 1976 Chevy Malibu. A $5,000 clunker that lasted a couple years until I could afford my next dream car: a 1970 Chevelle SS with gunmetal gray with black stripes with the words "strong styling" across the windshield. Best car I ever owned. Until this day, I wish I never sold it. One day I'll own another one—hopefully when I go through my mid-life crisis.

When I first had my Chevelle I met Chris Greco who had a Chevelle too. We started hanging out and working on each other's cars together. We became good high-school friends. He had a sister, Laurie, and a brother, Mikey. Mikey was always around us when we were fixing the cars or at the car meets in the Caldor parking lot. After a while, Laurie and I started dating. She hung out with her friends Gina and Diane, and her cousin Nancy. For years we all got along. Mikey was Laurie and I's sidekick every time we did something.

Sunday dinners with the family were remarkable. It was a special time in my life. One year, Laurie, Gina and I took a road trip to Disney World and had a blast. She still has some pictures of us from our adventures. Our relationship had no flaws—she was still in high school and I was working full time at a bagel shop. Our relationship grew, but then I started working different jobs at clubs and wanted to do my own thing, you know, acting like a selfish asshole. We started to grow apart; we never fought or trashed each other, but broke up after three and a half years. Never in a million years would I have thought we would fall back in love over thirty years later, but here we are with six kids and enjoying every minute I missed with her.

WORKING LIFE

At fourteen I got my first real job, a dishwasher at a place called Jewel's Restaurant in Toms River, NJ. I then became a short-order cook after six months and worked there for about a year. At sixteen, I started working at Marshalls as a stock person for about a year. After that, I worked at the bagel shop for several years. After that I started bouncing part time at various clubs in Seaside Heights, NJ. Then, I was working at some other bagel shops and go-go bars around the area for some extra money. I did this on and off until August of 1995 when I started my so-called career at a wire company.

I worked there until August of 2020, at which time I was laid off due to lack of work and the new virus going around: COVID-19. The virus has completely turned everybody's life upside down; it has shut places down, had everyone wearing masks in public, all schools went virtual, and many different products became hard to come by such as cleaning products, paper towels, toilet paper, Lysol, and most importantly hand sanitizer. It was a life changing experience for parents and the working class people. Lives were lost all around the world and people were going mad everywhere. The past two years have been life changing for every adult and child in the United States and all around the world. Basically the whole country was shut down —nobody leaving and nobody coming in. Until this day, October 2021, people are still wearing masks and seem afraid of each other hoping it will all end very soon.

SOMEONE SPECIAL TO ME I FORGOT - UNCLE JOHNNY

Growing up with an uncle that had Down Syndrome was interesting. He would always call me "Hitler" and my younger brother "Stromboli." For some reason he always tried to wrestle us. When we played music he would dance in a circle or bust out his keyboard. He was a very kind person when it came down to it; when I was dating Laurie, he would always say to me, "She's mine, get away, I love her," or "She doesn't like you anymore." He would say to my father, "When you gonna tip over, you?"

But when it came to his sister, my mother, forget about it; she could do no wrong. She quit school after 8th grade to take care of her brother full time and took care of him until the day he passed away. Nobody could ever fuck with him or she would get very pissed off and tell them how it was. She never held back on her words when it came to anything.

My brother Shawn always made video tapes of Johnny dancing around, talking to himself, whispering stuff to my brother and making hand gestures like hitting his chin, fixing the collars on his shirts or making noise with his mouth and grinding his teeth. He was a good man and had a lot of respect for others even though he wasn't "normal." We all treated him like anyone else and never different.

Gym Life

I remember working out at the Toms River Racketball Club with my boys, Joe Rabino and Bobby Ellis. The club had basketball courts, racket ball, wally ball, and plenty of weights to go around. One night, Bobby, Joe and I were doing dumbbell chest workouts. Bobby dropped the dumbbells and clipped his fingertip off! I had to drive his stick shift to the hospital for the first time; it was an experience.

We took a little break, but then a new gym opened up in our home town, Dynamic Fitness, which was more like a bodybuilding gym right between Jersey Mike's and the best Chinese restaurant ever; a downfall if you're trying to diet. Bobby, Joe and I started working out there and became really good friends with the owner, Vinny, and his friends Big Al, Ralph and Michelle, who were other clients. Some worked out for fun, and some for upcoming shows.

We all used to sit out in the parking lot and get high right before working out—best workouts at the time. It was the greatest feeling getting a good workout in a real gym. Some took it more seriously than others, but all-in-all, it was good times with good people. Dynamic was the best gym around for years. When the gym closed, Vinny opened another one not too far away, but it didn't have the same vibe as Dynamic did. Slowly, I stopped working out and started hanging out more.

CLUB LIFE

When we first got into clubs, neither of us drove except Bobby's one friend, Eddie B. He drove us everywhere in his 1970's Nova, which had a huge hole in the floor. When it came to clubbing, our favorite places were Lamour East, The Tunnel, Sound Factory, Hunka Bunka, The Coliseum, Electric Playground, Surf Club, The Chatter Box, Club X's, and Escape. I probably missed some clubs, but from what I remember those were the ones that left a good impression in my life and shaped me in the way I am today. We had a lot of great times at the club scene; it was an amazing time growing up in the 1980s and 1990s.

It was the best time for TV shows, music, movies, clubs and places to eat. I'm so glad I experienced those times. The new generation has no clue what life was like back in the days. We had no cell phones, no Xbox or Playstation, and no parents to get us out of trouble when something went wrong —you had to learn on your own. It's a different time now; kids are lazy and expect everything to be handed to them. They can't live without having their phones on them at all times. I really feel sorry for this generation. They all need a wakeup call. I've been very blessed in so many ways for my experiences while growing up.

GIRLS GROWING UP

I only had five serious girlfriends in my lifetime: two Tammys, Toni, Laurie and Valerie. Between them, I wound up only having one regret out of all five because my life would've been so much better than the way it was for the twenty plus years I was married, except for having my children. My regret was a girl named Laurie Greco, but we'll get back to her later on in the story.

In June of 1994, I got married to this girl I was only dating for about a year or so. Crazy now that I think about it. She was pretty cool with all my friends at the time and seemed like everyone liked her. We were total opposites from one another; she was a rocker chick and I was a hip-hop kind of guy. I liked freestyle, rap and deep house music. We didn't have that much in common besides the love of music. We bought our first house in the spring of

1996. A week later, I found out she'd been sleeping with one of my good friends of six years with no explanation other than "It just happened one night."

BACKTRACKING BEFORE I GOT MARRIED

I recall just before I got married that Laurie Greco wound up having a baby girl named Angela. She was maybe two months old when I went over to her parents' house. I was there to pay a debt I owed them for helping me out with some money—they were holding the title to my car until I paid them back. I told Laurie I was getting married. She looked saddened, but with a smile on her face, she asked if I wanted to hold Angela. She said I was the first guy besides her father, Frank, to hold her. So I did. She was so tiny and precious. I felt honored and I know now that I should've backed out of getting married and started over with Laurie.

Now Angela is twenty-eight years old and it's been over thirty years for Laurie and I, but we are a happy family with six kids in total and doing great. The times I spent with the Greco family were priceless and now they are even better. They always accepted me into their home and never gave up on me. I remember Laurie and her dad going to the mall looking for me. They were trying in different ways to show me I wasn't making the right choice by getting married. They knew I would be there because my soon-to-be wife worked at the mall as a hairdresser. Even my own father said, "I think you're making a big mistake." My mom always said that Laurie was the one for me and that she came from a good family. I always was family oriented until I got married—that should have been the first sign. Laurie tried her hardest to make me realize, but I never listened. I found out twenty-two years later that they were right. Wish I had followed all the signs then.

THE ROCKY ROAD AHEAD AFTER MARRIAGE

The day after we bought the house I threw her out for a year and stayed there alone. I thought about what I did wrong and couldn't come up with an answer. It was hard on me knowing the cheating was going on well before we even got married. Like a dummy, I took her back and ended my friendship with the kid I thought was my boy.

Things were good for a while after that. We went to a lot of concerts, did drugs, and after ten years had our first kid, Carlo. He wasn't really planned, but we worked it out. Carlo is eighteen now. Two years later, we had another kid, Lola, who is sixteen now. For some reason, eight years later, we had another one, Rocco, who is nine now. By the time Rocco was born, my wife was hooked on pills and I was constantly trying to help her get clean even though I found out she was still seeing my ex-friend behind my back saying they were just good friends and nothing else. Two years later we had our last kid, Luna, who is seven now.

To my ex-wife, drugs, drinking, boyfriend and other things were way more important than her family. When she was pregnant with Lola, she and I had a serious fight in front of Carlo. She ended up stabbing me in the arm in front of him and he still remembers what he was eating at the kitchen table and what happened that day. Carlo always asked me, "Dad, why did you stay all those years knowing what was going on behind your back, having more kids when she was doing nothing but torturing you and breaking your heart?" I tell him I can't explain it. Guess I thought this is what my life was supposed to be.

In June of 2015 we lost our house due to me trusting her with putting money in the bank, hoping everything was getting paid. I was wrong. We were eighteen months behind on our mortgage with no way out except to lose everything or move out of state to start over. At this point, we had nothing or nobody to back us up, and she drank all the time. I even found out that she left Rocco alone in the house when he was ten months old to get breakfast with the two older ones and then drive them to school. Her excuse was, "He was sleeping and that nothing was going to happen."

So I, with my bright ideas, quit my job of twenty years and moved to North Carolina to get my so-called wife away from all her friends and drugs to start over. The kids loved it there. They had new friends, a better home, and new schools. Unfortunately, it only lasted about five months before things got worse than they had been in New Jersey. The fights got bigger, things were getting broken every night, she would drink on the way home from work and would go to bars before coming home. She would have pills sent to the condo in the mail at least once a week. The cops were being called because of the noise. I wound up having to sleep on the floor next to Rocco every night because he was scared of his own mother all the time.

A week before Christmas 2015, I took the kids out of school when she went to work and we headed home to my mom's house not knowing the next step. She called begging and begging for us to come back because she said she was ready to change now. I had a sit-down with the kids and decided to go back not knowing what to expect. On Christmas Eve she took out all the presents in front of the kids and showed all of them what Santa was bringing them. The gifts were all unwrapped because she was drunk and fucked-up once again. At 4AM, she woke me up and said we had to wrap all the gifts before the kids got up. I said, "Why? You already showed them everything last night." She didn't remember anything from just a few hours ago, but we all did, so the gifts did not get wrapped.

The next day Lola came to me and told me, "Dad, I can't live like this anymore, we have to leave and go back to grandma's house." That was my breaking point. It broke my heart to hear how sad she was. Her, her baby sister and her brothers had seen so much stuff in their lives they never should've seen. And all because I was trying to fix a broken person that didn't care about anything in her life. The day after Christmas, a huge fight broke out between us. The cops came and they found out she was drunk through a breathalyzer test. They drove her to her father's house—about ten miles away from where we lived—and left her there. Hours after the cops dropped her off, her dad told her to get out and to take her problems with her, fix them, and not to come back until she did. "I don't want you coming here again," he told her. So she left with nobody knowing she had her car keys with her.

Back at the house, I ate dinner with the kids and put them to bed like usual. At 2AM, our dog started barking and there was knocking at the door. It was the police telling me that my wife got pulled over crossing into Virginia for reckless and drunk driving and was now in jail. She apparently told the cops she left the kids home alone so they were there to check on their well being. They had me wake each of them up so they could speak with the police. Finally, the cops left after about an hour and I had a talk with the kids.

The next morning, I went to buy a pack of smokes with my debit card and it didn't work. So I tried calling the bank and the phone didn't work either. Come to find out, before she got pulled over, she emptied the bank account and shut off all our phones because the account was in her name. She knew we didn't know anyone there or have any money to eat or leave. Then I got a call—I could receive calls, but not make any. It was the bail bonds asking if I would like to make bail for my wife and get her out of jail. I said no. He asked, "Really?" And again I said, "Really. I'm not bailing her out and don't call me again, bye," and hung up.

The next step was to call my mother-in-law and mother to get money transferred to me so we could leave. I started knocking on doors of people I didn't really know asking for help so I could make a phone call home. After I made the call and received the money, I rented a tow behind U-Haul and grabbed only what was important to the kids. The baby was only sixteen months. I grabbed the dog and never looked back. Everything else left behind was replaceable.

Of course when we returned to New Jersey, Social Services got involved right away—they were asking questions and interviewing all the kids. In the end, it was a no brainer for them. I finally did the right thing and got out of a dead-end relationship after twenty-two years and four kids. I'm really glad my Lola was part of my decision on not living the "toxic" life anymore.

BIG CITY DREAM

Out of all my friends, this kid Bobby Ellis AKA Big City, was my best friend since sophomore year of high school. Even though we went to different schools, we still lived in the same neighborhood growing up. I could remember hanging in my parents basement and DJing while he was beatboxing to my rhythm, going to surf club, chilling at the mall with our boomboxes and breakdancing on the street corners in Beachwood. Junior year for me, senior year for Bobby, we started working out together and smoking week with other kids from the neighborhood, like my boy Ray G and Rorre V, who we were tight with throughout the years.

When Bobby started driving, we would hit the strip in Seaside Heights where there were nice, classic and pimped out cars and loud music. As I started dating Laurie and we would all hang together. She would drive my Chevelle around Beachwood as Big City and I would be hotboxing the car while getting high. It was good times with each other and many fun times with Bobby. He had a Mitsubishi Precis hatchback—the "Big City Mobile." It had the baddest sound system around; everyone knew when he was pulling up.

As we got older, we would take trips to Oklahoma to visit Bobby's father every summer. It was a whole different world. We would go cat fishing with our hands, swim in the creeks and venture off looking at the flat lands. We also took many trips to New York City, buying mixed tapes, records, clothes and enjoying the club scene. I remember one time Bobby and I were riding our bikes in the snow and he fell over his handlebars because the snow and ice were bad and all in his spokes. Then, right before we got to my house, I fell and folded my tire in half—fucked up my whole bike. We used to take cabs from my house to go to the mall once in a while. One time, Mix Master

Mike and I were waiting at my house for Bobby in the cab and we ended up leaving Bobby behind only a block away—he was taking too long. He saw us pull away, but back then we didn't have cell phones so he got left behind. I remember taking New York City trips with Bobby, Joe and I to check out new clothes, sneakers, mix tapes or just to have a good time, but during this one trip, Bobby thought it would be funny to throw a firecracker in the toll. It flew back in the car between Joe's seat and his back and it went off! He was so pissed off at Bobby, but was okay; it ended up being a good trip anyway.

I remember Bobby driving my Chevelle to the city so we could go clubbing at The Sound Factory. There were a lot of crazy clubbers there. I think it had three floors, one for house, freestyle, and hip-hop where a guy with a four-piece drum set in the middle of the dance floor would bust out beats to the music. It was so amazing—you could listen for hours.

One day, my mother caught Bobby skinny dipping in my parents' pool at like 2AM. My mom was like, "Bobby, what are you doing? Don't you know it's late? Get out." After that, I don't think it happened again, but Big City was like family at that point. His mother used to make the best homemade egg rolls and this stuff called Siopao, a Filipino steamed dumpling— to die for. Big City also was a somewhat master with the numb chucks and the samurai sword. I'm pretty sure he was a black belt in Karate. The kid was a beast. Always had my back. My memories with him will never be forgotten. I had some of my best times with Big City. He was even my best man when I got married; true friends to this day.

LOSING MY PARENTS

My father and I had a wonderful relationship. Growing up, I could remember family gatherings and parties with family and friends. In May of 1999, the day before Memorial Day, my father had asked me to come over, clean up the yard and take him to get a new grill—he wanted to have everyone over for a BBQ the next day. We hung out for a couple of hours, took care of everything and he kept saying to me it was the best he's ever felt in years. He was in such good spirits.

He went on to eat lunch with my mom and I reached home. I got home, jumped in the shower and the phone rang. It was my mother. Hysterically, she was screaming that dad had finished his lunch, fell back in his chair and wasn't breathing. I jumped out of the shower and drove as fast as I could over to the house. The ambulance and cops were there working on him, rushed him to the hospital and overnight had to revive him four times. The only thing keeping him alive was a machine. They told us he was already brain dead and asked us to decide on what we wanted to do. We had no choice then to let him go in peace.

He wouldn't have wanted to be a vegetable for the rest of his life. We had to pull the plug. It was the hardest thing I've ever had to do, especially knowing he felt the "best ever" that day.

My mother was a one-of-a-kind person. Never cared about hurting anyone's feelings. She was very blunt and upfront with everything. We were close until March of 2020; it was then that she was diagnosed with Dementia and Covid-19 at the same time. Nobody out of the four boys could take her in for living arrangements. The state wound up taking care of her until the day she died in June of 2021. Nobody was allowed to see her from the time they took her because of the virus. She died all alone which saddened me and hurts knowing she was always there for me and nobody was there for her. She was like my rock in so many ways.

A SHOCKING SURPRISE

About five years after my father passed away, my aunt Susie called me to tell me she   had something very important to tell me. She asked if I was sitting down and then she proceeded, "I want you to know that you have a sister that's a year older than your brother Shawn. She lives in Long Branch and has lived there her whole life (which is only about forty-five minutes from where I lived my whole life.) Her name is Tammy Sorenson and we're having a family reunion this summer. We would like for you and Shawn to come meet her." I was blown away, especially since she didn't live that far away.

So my wife, my two kids and I met up with my brother, his wife and kids at my cousin Billy's house up north somewhere—can't remember the town—but it was about a four-hour trip. My aunt Susie, her new husband Mike, and all of my cousins were there except for Susan who I haven't seen since I was fifteen. It was time to meet my sister and her parents. I was mind blown. She had my father's eyes and jawline. You could tell she was family by her looks. Her parents were so friendly. Meeting my dad's girlfriend was cool, I could tell why he had a connection with her. It was one of the best times in my life, being together with everyone. After it was over, I kept in touch with my sister for about a year. She then moved to Colorado and had a baby after she got married. It was nice to have met her and to know she was good friends with my aunt.

THE STORM OF THE CENTURY - SUPERSTORM SANDY

I remember the storm hit on my daughter, Lola's, ninth birthday in 2012. My ex-wife's father was up from North Carolina for a visit. It was October, the wind picked up shortly after the power went out and we tried celebrating as best we could. Then, we all tried going to bed; everyone was scared because there was a lot of noise outside and nobody knew what to expect the next day. We got up the next morning to the basement flooded, trees down everywhere, and the biggest one from our yard leaning up against the house. The water from the bay, which was four blocks from us, was now half a block away. Still no power and the state was basically crippled. So my ex-wife's father started packing up—he wanted to get out of the state before getting stuck staying with us (he was never a good father figure). So he left. We all gathered our flashlights together, brought in as much firewood for the wood burning stove which would now be our only source of heat. We used it to warm up bottles for the baby, Rocco, and to make whatever food we could on the top of it.

A week went by and still no power. The state was still shut down everywhere. Hardly any gas available because trucks couldn't make deliveries. Things were getting harder and harder to get and to deal with, especially with having a wife who had a drug problem and three kids. So I took a ride to my mother's house who I hadn't spoken with in a while, and asked her if my family could stay with her after explaining that we'd been out of power for a week and things had been hard with the kids. She agreed to let us come stay, so I went back home and got everyone ready to leave. Once at my mom's house, all five of us got to set up in one room. Grateful to have food, heat, electricity and bathrooms that work, it was better for the whole family and much safer.

Things were manageable until Carlo and Lola came home with lice from playing with the kids across the street. My ex was dozing off all the time with the baby, my mother was finally saying something to her about it, and then next thing you know, my ex-wife wanted to go home to "ride it out." Ultimately, we only lasted about four days at my mom's house. She was heartbroken having us leave because she was worried about her grandkids.

Back at the war zone, the tree was still leaning on the house, other trees were all over the neighborhood laying across roads, people's lawns, and against other trees just waiting to fall down. Twelve days after the storm, there was still no power in many parts of the state. I got more firewood from my neighbor, Brian, and a generator for the food and coffee maker. It lasted for a total of twenty-one days without power. It was the hardest thing to go through with the kids, but we survived it, barely. We were lucky to have a lot of help from friends and neighbors.

At this point, my ex-wife's mother needed a place to stay because her house was being raised and fixed due to water damage, plus her friends couldn't help her out anymore. So she came to stay with us. That didn't last too long because her daughter was always fucked up and was acting out of control, even more than normal. One day, my ex thought it was a good idea to get out and embarrass her mother in front of the neighbors by saying some hurtful things. She ended up telling her to leave, even though she knew her mother had nowhere else to go. It was a time I tried to forget about because it was my home and the neighbors were in shock, but at least they knew what I was up against and they tried helping me in any way they could. It took a long time before everything was almost back to normal, years, actually. I still keep in touch with Brian and Rob, who were the best neighbors anyone could ever ask for. God bless them always for looking out for my family and I.

MAKING MY LAST TRIP

I was going back to North Carolina to get my DJ equipment, records, the kids' bikes, things from our storage unit, and some things from the condo. I asked one of my good friends, Phil Jackson, if he would like to take the journey with me for some help, and also because I didn't know what to expect when getting the kids' bikes from my ex father's house. He always blamed me for bringing my problems to his house when he knew it was all of his daughter's fault since she couldn't control her bad habits. Phil and I got there, picked up the tow behind U-Haul, and headed over to the storage unit. We grabbed my two turntables, mixer, speakers, twelve milk crates of records, all my son's legos, my fishing poles, and most of the kids' important things that I couldn't grab the first time. Then, we grabbed some lunch at Arby's and headed over to the condo where everything was already packed up from my ex. When she came back with her twenty-two year long relationship boyfriend, she could just come get it when they were ready.

We evaluated how much room we had left and what would fit knowing we still had to grab the kids' bikes and Rocco's prized big red car from the TV show "The Wiggles." We tried to make sure we picked up things that would benefit the kids. I took some things from the condo, but I should've taken my time and taken anything worth money, because she had drained everything we had saved up. It would've been easy too; everything was labeled, but I wasn't thinking clearly and was hoping to get out of there with no problems as we did. Until we got to her dad's house. His new wife was sitting outside cursing up a storm and talking shit about me. The bikes were at the end of the driveway and she yelled to me to "hurry the fuck up and get out of here before Jerry comes out of the house and fucking shoots you with his gun now."

I looked at Phil and we put everything on the

roof racks and drove out of the neighborhood away from her dad's house to tie them down for a safe trip home. It was a thirteen hour drive with a lot of amazing views, and we made it home safely without any problems. All in all, I could understand her father's hatred towards me because he finally got to see and live around his grandkids, and then they were gone. He needed to hold his daughter accountable for that, not just me. I wanted my kids to be safe and away from all the bullshit, so that's what I did.

HOW LAURIE AND I RECONNECTED-
THE FINAL CHAPTER

The week before I moved to North Carolina, I was at the local food store, ShopRite, and ran into my only regret in life: Laurie Greco, and her son, Sean. I hadn't seen her in over twenty plus years, even though we lived really close to each other. When I came home from moving, January 2016, we started talking about a rumor I had heard that she and my ex-wife were best friends on Facebook. Come to find out, Laurie didn't even have an account. So we talked, she told me she was happy in her marriage, and she started coming over to see the kids so they had some kind of mom figure in their life. Then, my son Carlo brought a kid from school over to my mom's house and became good friend with him. It was Laurie's son, Sean, which neither of us had a clue. After about four or five months, she finally told me she wasn't happy in her marriage and didn't know what to do. I told her I was there for her no matter what, if she wanted to talk, but I didn't want to be in the middle between her and her husband, or be the cause of her leaving him.

Until she filed for her divorce, we talked for a while because she wanted to try making things work between them, but in the end nothing she did or said was working out. After that, things between us were great. It felt like we had never broken up and that we started where we left off. We'd never fight or yell at each other, or even put each other down. Total support in every way. She accepted my kids as her own and I did the same. To this day, we have our disagreements about stuff, but nothing we can't talk through in a normal way. Laurie helped me with my ex-wife because we had joint custody and it never wired out. Twelve out of fifteen weekends she would get drunk to where I would have to pick them back up. I tried for months to be civil, but she ended up leaving to stay at a halfway house in Philly and never looked back. It's been almost six years since the babies talked to her or even saw her.

Even with a court order for child support, nothing at all. Since our divorce, she received two lawsuits that were at least $10,000 a piece and still hasn't made one single payment. She just took care of her own needs. Her own mother kept her ring and hocked it. She didn't give the kids any money because her daughter, apparently, owed her money. Funny thing about life is that the kid who wanted me to leave all of it, Lola, is the only one who has had a phone relationship with her mother for the past year. But she's slowly learning that some people don't change and that her mother is still in the same spot she was in six years ago, except now she has a dog and a cat that she cares for instead of her own children.

Since we walked away, things changed for the better: I've been with the love of my life, bought a new house with a pool, all the kids call her mom, and we are both doing great all around. I couldn't ask for a better partner to live the rest of my life with. My kids and I are truly blessed to be where we are today after everything that has happened.

FINAL WORDS AND LAST THOUGHTS

Throughout my whole story, I've never once said that I was an angel. I did drugs along with my ex-wife for a period of time, I fought with her back and forth in front of my kids, and I did some stupid shit, but I never put anything before my kids or my bills. I never crossed the line in my relationship, until I had no choice. I never left the kids alone anywhere, and I never spent money on drugs before my family. Still, I never said I was the perfect husband or father. The worst thing I did while my kids were around was smoke weed. It may not have been right, but that's my truth.

Till this day, even though my ex wife still won't admit it, my ex and my ex-friend are together in some way, but not the whole time we were married. Some people might say that all those kids aren't mine, but I've been there since the beginning and I'll be there until the day I die without any worries.

My journey in life and what my family has been through might not connect with anyone, but if I can help one guy out there that's going through the same situation as I was with little kids and sees that it can be done, then it was worth it to me to tell my story.

"The Life of Chuck" - Thank you.

CPSIA information can be obtained
at www.ICGtesting.com
Printed in the USA
LVHW051055070322
712798LV00007B/424

9 781088 020531